"When Two or Three"

"When Two or Three"

David Bullock

For my wife, Claudia,
who gives and grows my purpose through her
love.
And to the memory of Ann Satterfield,
may her call to Spiritual Direction inspire others.

CONTENTS

FOREWORD ix
PREFACE xii
ACKNOWLEDGEMENTS xv

Introduction 1

You Can't Do It Alone 7

one Build Your Circle 11

two Consider a Professional 21

Making Decisions 31

three Money's a Matter 33

four Discernment 37

Introducing Spirituality 43

five How Can We Be More Spiritual? 49

six Finding A Spiritual Director 57

seven Religious Congregations and Clergy 63

eight   Working With A Coach to
              Find Spiritual Purpose   65

nine   Meeting with a Faith-Based
                     Therapist   69

                     Conclusion   72

                          Notes   75

ABOUT THE AUTHOR   79

Foreword

Life can be hard. We all face challenges, uncertainties, and moments of doubt that can make it difficult to find our way. A spiritual anchor—a sense of deeper meaning and connection—can provide the grounding we need in these turbulent times. While discovering your purpose may not always make life easier, it does bring a sense of direction, making the journey through life's waves more meaningful and, dare I say, even more enjoyable.

I met David while I was taking spiritual direction coursework during seminary, on my way to becoming an Episcopal priest. I sort of fell into taking the classes; it was a tumultuous time at the school, and these classes were a respite filled with practical skills, deep listening, meaningful silence, and tools for making choices in life that lead to greater wholeness and thriving.

As I got to know David through these courses, I was struck by his dedication to guiding others on this journey of meaning and purpose. When we reconnected and I learned he was working as a coach, it made perfect sense, as we share the understanding that wellness involves our whole selves, and this holistic endeavor makes the most sense in a context that considers all aspects of wellness: not just physical and mental wellness, but emotional, spiritual, relational, financial, and vocational wellness—all the parts of ourselves that make up our identities and that we live out in the day-to-day.

These components of wellness are all interwoven, but we can attend to some more than others based on our culture, personality, or any number of factors. The role and impact of spirituality is one that can be overlooked, yet can have a profound impact on overall wellness. I believe David appreciates this, and his passion and value for holistic well-being and for the flourishing that can happen in a life of groundedness and purpose come through in his book.

"When Two or Three" integrates coaching knowledge with valuable spiritual practices, insights for those seeking greater meaning and purpose, and areas like vocation and personal finance that may not immediately read as spirituality, but have spiritual resonance and impact nonetheless. This book is designed to help you uncover your true purpose and weave spirituality into the rigors daily life. It offers a way to not just understand your spiritual needs but to actively engage with them as you move forward on your growth journey.

Whether you are someone seeking something more on your journey to wellness or you are a coach looking for more resources or education around spirituality and spiritual practices, this book is a practical toolbox for incorporating greater wellness by focusing on spirituality. David balances his perspective from specific spiritual traditions with broadly accessible spiritual concepts, and encourages readers to delve deeper into their inner lives while making tangible progress toward their goals.

I appreciate the thoughtful way David has brought together ancient wisdom and contemporary practice. Whether you are a coach seeking to deepen your practice or someone beginning to explore the spiritual dimension of your life, this book will serve as an interesting introduction and faithful companion on your journey, and I hope that it opens the door to greater hope, joy, and wellbeing along your journey.

The Rev. Alissa G. Anderson

Preface

Thank you for picking up this book. I hope you are looking to find purpose in your life, and have considered to do so with a spiritual mindset. If so, this book should help you find what you are meant to do or your calling. It should answer the question, "Why am I here?" And that concept is one that is radical, but the results to answering that question doesn't need to be so radical at all. By engaging in the process outlined in this book, you should find the change you need, even if it is as simple as spending more time with family or reading fiction more. Life should be what it calls you to do. It should be geared toward what you love to do.

The drive to write this book came out of a need I saw in health and wellness coaching. I had a background in Spiritual Direction before I passed my boards to become a National Board Certified Health and Wellness coach. I understood from the training I received to pass the boards that spirituality was an important part of looking at a person holistically in coaching practice. However, there were very few resources covering the topic in both the training of health and wellness coaches and for the continuing education of this type of coach.

As a result, I intended this book to be for a general audience, but also one in which coaches could recommend the book to their clients who were looking to find their purpose or calling in life, but through a spiritual lens. There is not much literature on the topic and I thought it would be enjoyable and productive to fill that vacant niche.

The book talks about the steps you need to take in order to find your purpose or calling in life. I start with identifying the people on your spiritual team that you would need to work with to find your purpose or calling.

The need to find people to commune with is ever more important. Even if the relationship is secular. My alma mater, Bates College, has a nationally recognized program for its students called, The Center for Purposeful Work. Dr. Allen W. Delong, Senior Associate Dean for Purposeful Work at Bates, engages with his students to find out what they would like to pursue and if that call fits into the alignment of who they are and what they want to be.

But to matters of spirituality sometimes Delong refers students to the Chaplain of Bates College, the Rev. Dr. Brittany Longsdorf. Like one of the major messages of this book, she agrees that reaching out to others to find community as a spiritual tool is important. Longsdorf has found that more often students are preparing to look to maintain community after leaving college for the working world. She noted that, "More seniors are making moving decisions after college based on relationships," rather than going to someplace solely to find a particular type of work or being close to home. People are becoming the more important motivator in finding a purpose or calling.

In this book, I then move on to the topics of money and of the discernment process, in which the importance of decision-making is outlined. Finally, I wrap up the book with a brief summary of spirituality and the people you would need to work with in order to better embrace the spiritual into your life.

I hope this is what you are looking for. Some of the points made in the book may seem obvious, but I am sure there are some parts that you may have not considered. I hope you benefit from reading it as much as possible.

Acknowledgements

No work is done alone. I try to emphasize this point in this text early on and in the title. I want to thank my wife for supporting me so much throughout my training as a Health and Wellness Coach and as a Spiritual Director. She is truly the person I am meant to be with and she is always at my side. I love her so much and I appreciate the love she gives and continues giving to me. I also would like to thank General Theological Seminary and the Mayo Clinic for giving me the training and rigor to have the background to write this book, but to also the ability to do the research and background investigation needed to put pen to paper. I want to thank the people at the Bates Center for Purposeful Work and the Rev. Dr. Brittany Longsdorf of the Bates College Multi-faith Chaplaincy, for giving insight into those individuals making one of their first attempts at finding one's calling in life and how that process is changing. I also want to thank my Spiritual Directors, I-Fong Wu and Louise Litke for getting me closer to God through both times of light and times of darkness. Thanks should go out to my Spiritual Direction Supervision group. Edgardo Lugo runs a great group every month and I feel blessed that I found out about them through SDI. Returned blessings should go out to the churches I have gone to throughout the years, including Our Saviors Lutheran, Saint Anselm, Messiah Lutheran, Christus Rex, Saint Peter's Lexington, The Church of the Good Shepherd, Advent Lutheran, The Church of Saint Matthew and Saint Timothy, First Evangelical Lutheran, and Saint Mary Magdalene's

Church. I also appreciate all the coaches and therapists I've had over the years. They have helped me accomplish much and emphasized the structure I needed to be the person I always wanted to be. I want to shout out to the National Board of Health and Wellness Coaches. Thank you for expanding my profession, from the administrative work you do to the webinars and events that promote the profession. Thank you to my family, Bullock, Rigby, Murphy, Delano, De Maria and Ricardo. You have all supported me so much, from my first articles and books on space and space exploration, a trend which I am not finished with, to the spiritual path I have also taken on in midlife. No one could have done all I've done without you all. Thank you to my editor, the Rev. Alissa Goudswaard Anderson, who also wrote the Foreword for this book. Her work on bringing this piece closer to publishing well is due her credit. And thanks be to God, my Higher Power, His Son and the Holy Spirit, who guide me throughout my days with prayer.

Introduction

So You Want to Find Spiritual Meaning and Purpose in Your Life

"I know you understand it all. So why don't I get back on my feet again?" - Jeremy Camp

Have you ever felt like something important is missing from your life, even though you've tried to fill the void? Maybe you've explored self-help books, dabbled in different faith practices, or focused on improving your health—but still, that sense of purpose eludes you. Perhaps you find yourself wondering, "Is this really what I'm meant to be doing?" Whether it's something that permeates your whole life or is concentrated in your relationships, your work, or how you spend your free time, the questions linger. What if spirituality could be the missing piece you've been searching for? What if it could help you feel more grounded, more connected, and lead you toward the life you've always wanted? This book is your guide to discovering untapped spiritual resources and revisiting familiar ones with fresh eyes, all to set you on a journey of profound self-discovery of what you are meant to do. It's time to explore, and perhaps uncover, the better version of yourself that's waiting to be found.

Anyone who reads this book in its entirety will find something to learn about their spiritual calling from reading it, no matter what background. No matter what belief system, creed, religion or lack thereof, can benefit. This is because there are secular and universal truths to spirituality and also there are secular and universal truths to finding purpose in your life. That said, some of the content in this book is not secular. Judeo-

Christian, Islamic, Taoist and Buddhist points of view along with glimmers of inspiration from these faiths are just some of the content from specific belief systems that are presented, as well. As much as the world can seem like it is tearing apart, note that in most places in the world, at any one point in time, there is relative peace. Together, we can seek to tap into that peace with this book.

Chances are that exploring spirituality and making change will have a positive impact in your life. Spirituality in practice and in almost all forms has been scientifically studied, especially most recently. Although the incoming data is encouraging, it is not complete. However, it can be easily said that there are both physical and mental health benefits to becoming more spiritual. Becoming more spiritual and religious can even help you become more resilient in a neighborhood with adverse conditions. (1)

Becoming more spiritual fills emotional and religious voids in many people's lives. It gives answers to questions that deepen a mystery at times and yet unlike science that yearns for truth, spirituality can give a response of "both-and." Not one way *or* the other, but *both* one way *and* another. In these situations, where there are no absolutes, studies have proved that the comfort in believing in the spiritual mystery is beneficial psychologically for those who come to its radical conclusion.

For example, Buddhists believe that enlightenment is found when one realizes that "life is suffering." How can enlightenment and pain be simultaneous? To turn to science: entities on the quantum scale are both particle and wave. How can something be both a particle and a wave? Christians believe that God, Jesus, and the Holy Spirit comprise the Holy Trinity, meaning that they are both one God and three separate, coequal entities at the same time. How can this be? How can the three be one? Learning to trust in mysteries teaches us that we don't need to have all the answers and that's ok.

In fact, as neuroscientist and MD Andrew Newberg posits in his book *Neurotheology: How Science Can Enlighten Us About Spirituality*, religions "offer effective ways of coping with the uncertainties of the world. Religions provide a sense of control, helping us understand when we should plant or harvest crops and how to avoid specific dangers such as floods. Religions can provide answers to ontological questions about the meaning and purpose of life, thereby reducing 'ontological anxiety.'" (2)

Science and Spirituality

While spiritual-religious mysteries offer profound insights, it's also valuable to explore how science intersects with our understanding of spirituality. By examining the relationship between science and spirituality, we can gain a more holistic perspective on the changes we experience. Let's begin by exploring the difference between correlational and causal relationships, key concepts in scientific research and ways of understanding cause and effect. This is an important clarification because most scientific measurements of change between individual subjects who experience spiritual, mental or emotional change are correlational relationships, not causal relationships.

Correlational relationships in science are those in which there are two variables, but a change in one variable does not mean a change in the other variable is a direct influencer of the resulting change. The relationship between violence on television and crime is an example of this: imagine violence on television for a particular TV viewership has increased over time, and crime spikes among that viewership during the same period. Two variables changed, but there is no way to prove that violence on television and increased crime are directly related to each other. How the mind is affected by some sort of influence is difficult to measure between two indirect variables. The relationship between the minds of a population that watches TV and violence that coincides is a correlational relationship, where one variable cannot be proven to be in a direct relation to the other. Correlational relationships occur often in psychology and the study of the mind, and while we needn't always discount correlational relationships in scientific study, we should realize that the relationship is not a direct one.

For a causal relationship, let's look to physics. A relationship in which one event causes the other can be seen in the example of driving a car. If someone puts their foot down on the gas pedal, the car will accelerate. One action causes another. There is no question about it. In a causal relationship, one variable can be proven to cause another, demonstrating a direct relationship between the variables.

Because spirituality is so intertwined with psychology, we should be inclined to look to data and research, but data and research only go so far. An example often used is the concept of a placebo in religion and spirituality (R/S). One could say that there is no proof of a causal relationship between performing a spiritual practice and experiencing a measurable positive result or effect—thus the spiritual practice is a placebo and the result a placebo effect. This is an easy challenge to counter: if the placebo fixes or positively affects the subject, why discount it? Problem fixed. It may make sense to just keep the practice despite the lack of proof.

With advances in technology and research, studies of R/S and health show an increased causal relationship between the two variables. (3) The use of fMRIs and EKGs is shedding some light on the relationship between R/S and the mind. These studies are showing that incorporating spirituality makes a significant difference to one's life journey. We will look at the relationship between health and spirituality and why being in good health is important to finding one's purpose.

A Topic of Many Gifts

This book is also one book of many on the subject of spiritual meaning and purpose. Some of my favorite authors on the topic include Parker Palmer, Meagan Driscoll and Dr. Dharius Daniels. Sacred texts, such as the Bible, the Torah and the Koran are also good sources of inspiration for those seeking spiritual purpose. Poets such as Rumi and Mary Oliver can speak to the heart. And there are so many more—more texts and practices than could ever be included in a single book. I would like to emphasize that to find a book to read, one should go about it spiritually, too. Find a book that speaks to you when you are looking to find your purpose. Don't take it as an assignment from school or work. Listen to your heart when you are seeking the right book to find your purpose.

In other words, if you can find a connection with another outlet on the topic of this book, go for it. There are many, many sources of spiritual inspiration. Being more spiritual is about finding the light, life and love inside. It's about making positive connections. If something draws you into it and it is good, embrace it. You may have something special. This is finding a calling, and your calling should tell you where to go.

A Taiwanese study looked at spiritual leadership and its relationship with the well-being or calling of over 150 nurses. According to data based on nurses' answers to interview questions, the correlation between those who said they had a spiritual relationship in their work and those who names well-being or calling in their attitude at work was strong. (4) In other words, the nurses who found their work to be spiritual also said that they found their work to enhance their well-being and made them feel they were pursuing a calling.

The Latin root for vocation is *vox*—literally voice—and the verb form *vocare* means "to call." If we listen we can hear the voice of our calling. As poet and essayist Parker Palmer points out, "Vocation does not come from a voice 'out there' calling me to be something I am not. It comes from a voice 'in here' calling me to be the person I was born to be, to fulfill the original selfhood given to me at birth by God." (5) So listen to the voice inside, you may be surprised.

Palmer also adds that finding your calling may not come from knocking on a door and having it open, like the maxim, "if you knock a door will open." Contrastingly, Palmer learned throughout the opportunities in his life that opportunities may come from weighing your options after a door closes.

But how do you become more spiritual? How do you find purpose and identify calling? Read on. The journey awaits.

Putting God First

Now that you are ready to take those first steps, what should you do first? I suggest you put your relationship with a Higher Power first. How do you do this? First, let me explain what I mean by Higher Power.

The term Higher Power comes from the peer support organization of Alcoholics Anonymous (AA) groups. AA is a very popular recovery program among people with a substance abuse disorder, and its structure and methodology has been expanded to other mutual help organizations, going beyond substance abuse to things like eating disorders. AA is not perfect, and it is not for everyone, but for many people, AA is a practice that works.

AA is a system that helps people get sober around the world, and not just get sober but stay sober. One of the reasons people commit to sobriety is because as part of the practice of AA, they submit to a Higher Power.

A Higher Power can be defined as God, Allah, Jehovah, Jesus, Father, Mother, the Goddess, the Divine, or whatever title you wish to give. Higher Power actually came into use as a term that transcended religion and could speak to atheists. When the predominately Christian practice of AA was brought to Poland during the Cold War, the Polish government was run by atheist communists, and they needed to find a term that those in AA could relate to. It had to be something like an all-encompassing God, but not a religious term. Higher Power was used because it was something they could relate to and a term that would be accepted, and it caught on throughout the world.

This book uses the term Higher Power in an attempt to be more universally relatable, but sometimes I will use God, Jesus, and the names of other religious figures for impact and emphasis. Feel welcome to substitute your own preferred term or name at any point.

So put God first. And be intentional about it. What does it mean to be intentional? If you make the effort to pray, meditate, listen, or just try to be at peace, you are in the process of being intentional in that practice. Intention could be translated into any action as well. Not just a solitary one, such as prayer. Making that first step is important even if you end up failing or lapsing from whatever you were intentional about. Nike said it right, "Just Do It." It's ok. Because whatever you do, a Higher Power is watching, listening and planning for you too.

You Can't Do It Alone

"For where two or three gather in my name, there am I with them." Matthew 18:20

Before diving in to the nuts and bolts of spirituality, rituals, and heart-listening for the point of finding your calling, we must consider something important about process. One of the most important things I've learned is that to do anything spiritual, you must not go about it alone. In fact, I would suggest that anything, even if it is not spiritual, should be done in community. In fact, it's hard not to: even outside of spiritual practice, you still have to eat, house, and trade with others. Some of us may find that more appealing than others, but even as solitary practitioners living in happy introversion, there are books to be read by authors who took time to connect with their audience. And in fact, relationships with others are one of the major ways we connect with a Higher Power.

Matthew 18:20, in the Christian Bible, tells us that even if we pray to God alone, to call on him we need to have others. This concern for others is the basis of Jesus's second commandment: the first being to love the Lord God with all your heart and all your soul, the second to love your neighbor as yourself. This request for love is the center of all that Jesus taught.

Putting people first in your life is a way of putting a Higher Power first. Most or even all of these people don't need to practice spiritually with you, all they need to do is support you and your journey, just as you are.

It is also important, when you are alone and in prayer, that you pray for others as well. You can repent, give thanks and worship God alone in prayer, but it is also good to pray for others and their health and wishes, and to practice forgiveness in prayer.

According to David De Steno in his book, *How God Works: The Science Behind the Benefits of Religion*, he writes," When it comes to physical illness, social ties also play an important role. Loneliness contributes to a host of maladies, including viral illness, heart disease, diabetes, sleep disorders, hypertension and depression." (6)

So when you find someone to spiritually connect with, talk about what you want to do with your life. Find your purpose with them. It could be starting a new business, or it could be that you found that you want to spend more of your free time quilting. The Dialogue with Your Future is there. You simply need to explore.

Who do we talk to about our purpose? Part I is divided into two chapters. The first chapter is dedicated to finding those from your support circle who can help you in your spiritual journey. These are familial people. The other group outlined in Chapter Two focuses more on paid professionals and paid events where you can find others. You can be successful at finding your calling with just one person, or you can have a whole army of generals, friends, and acquaintances who are there for you and where you need to go. God is calling and I suggest you do not go about this alone.

One

Build Your Circle

"What is a friend? A single soul dwelling in two bodies." - *Aristotle*

If you're going to make great changes in your life, you are going to need support. If you respect that others who support you are going to need help experiencing changes in their life, or if they plan on making changes themselves, you are going to need to support others. And what you do for others, you will learn from for yourself, too.

Independence is good, but people need people. As much as one can try to get off the grid and be more independent when it comes to spirituality, our ministry is to share and commune. This is not about governmental politics. This is different. This has to do with spirituality and religion. It's not about rights, government policy or any of that type of decision-making, but it is political because it is about heart directed decision making. This about making decision and taking action with the politics of "You." People were never meant to be alone. Let's focus on that now.

Starting with Family

So how do we commune with others spiritually? Family is the best place to start—whether that is family of origin or family of choice. Your family consists of long-term relationships that are known to you. Chances are, you have been connected to your family since birth, and chances are, you are in a family that loves you as well. For those of us who are married, a spouse is a partner in the family dynamic that should have your full support and encouragement, not only out of love but also through your mutual commitment. Children can not only be a source of supportive joy, but a supportive commitment as well. Siblings may be the only people who have seen you throughout all of the changes of your life and may know you the longest—don't be afraid to reach out to them for spiritual support as well.

For American society, the nuclear family is the most recognized unit for familial relationships. Legally, more so than your friends, if the government, such as a social worker or the police wants to find out more about you, they tend to reach out to your family first. We may be compelled to deny family for whatever reason, but the ties to our family are very strong by society's standards as well.

You may feel uncomfortable reaching out to family to support you on your journey for change and purpose. They might not want you to change your job, move, or both, which is understandable, but they can also be a source of resources to find out the spiritual traditions of your family. One example of this is knowing who your ancestors are: many faith traditions invite prayer not only to a Higher Power, but to ancestors as well. Another thing you can learn is how has faith changed from generation to generation within the family. For those with a family business, you may want to talk to your family for advice on how the business has changed over the years, how they do the work they do and how the work done has changed over the years. These questions can help you find your purpose or calling.

There are other questions you can ask. Can you pray with your family? Would you want to attend a religious service with your family? Would it be easy or hard to talk to your family about the details of your life and your relationship with a Higher Power? Would they want to listen? Would listening be a shared spiritual experience in and of itself? There is no right or wrong way to engage your family in your spiritual journey, but these questions may provide a place to start.

After considering familial support, you might turn for support on your spiritual journey to your friends.

On to Friends

Friends are people in your life that you shared with, that you've walked with, that you've accomplished things with, and that you've simply had fun with. Good friends are there when you need them most. Even though some friends may just be acquaintances to you, that is fine, too. Every relationship can be cherished.

What is important spiritually, is this question. Could you talk to a friend about your spiritual experiences? Could you share non-spiritual—or spiritual—experiences and explorations with them? Could you pray together? Could you go on retreat together? Hike in nature together? Simply look at the stars and wonder together about something greater than ourselves?

Friends can be soulmates on the spiritual journey, and the spiritual journey can also spark and grow friendships Although, will the same people who are your soulmates, be willing to talk about your calling? You need to find out someone who will talk with you about purpose.

Peers Support

"Peers" are similar to friends, and have some overlap, but are also somewhat different and distinct. These are people you connect with based on a shared identity. They could be friends or acquaintances and could be support, even spiritual support.

Peers are found in support groups (e.g. AA), other health groups, political groups, church groups, or other membership-based nonprofits. Peer groups could meet online or in person.

An example of a peer group could be a choir or acapella group. A group like this typically meets in person with a shared identity of being singers, while bringing together people from different backgrounds. Among any group of peers, you may find people to share a spiritual experience or willing to support you on a spiritual journey of transformation. Your quest for spiritual meaning could be the rallying cry for the whole group, or could be from just one person in that group.

Peer groups have the potential to foster long-term relationships or short-term relationships, are readily available on social media (and often communicate via social media regardless of setting), and could support intimate conversation.

Find it in the House of the Lord

Another place where supportive relationships can form is in houses of worship. Not only that, but houses of worship are places where you can connect to a Higher Power both by yourself and with others. Houses of worship typically foster connection and transformation through prayer and worship (religious services and prayer groups), study and learning (Bible studies or religious education), service and action (volunteering with outreach ministries such as soup kitchens or getting involved in leadership), and life together (social events or small groups). Ritual, an important facet for growing spirituality, is readily available in houses of worship. Even the physical spaces can connect you with the majesty and wonder of God. Many houses of worship are beautiful, and most have a history. Involvement with houses of worship remind us that we are connected to one another and something larger.

Participation in houses of worship is also good for mental health: religious involvement has been shown to decrease the ideation of suicide in the elderly (7), and a study during the COVID-19 lock-downs showed that religious involvement, even if virtual, bettered mental health for congregants in the population studied. (8)

As much as attending houses of worship provides positive health benefits, though, it's okay if you feel uncomfortable participating. Religious service attendance is not required to be spiritual in your life or for finding your spiritual purpose. This is why we need to have other people in our life to find purpose and meaning and to be more spiritual—for example, our coworkers.

Work It

People we work with can also be a source of support in many ways. Colleagues are people at work with whom you have a relationship, be it inside of work, outside of work, or both. Working side-by-side naturally leads to socializing, and this work relationship is something to embrace and celebrate. Make an effort to go to work functions and celebrations, and try to talk to your colleagues. Although not spiritual, this practice is good for the spirit and can help you spiritually, and celebrations tend to have a generally spiritual bent.

Talking to your colleagues about your personal spiritual merits consideration. It's important to set boundaries at work, and you want to be absolutely sure a colleague would want to share spiritual insights before broaching the subject. If the work relationship is one that crosses over into friendship, being open can be easily understandable, but some people like to keep work at work and save the personal for after work—nothing wrong with that.

Finding your purpose, though, is ideal at work. What you do there helps you find out what you want to do in the future. You have resources at work that could help you out. Help can come in the form of a benefits package, an Employee Assistance Program (EAP), or continuing education. The changes in your life you track that you uncover and pursue to find your purpose could even mean that the changes you need to do are so flexible that you may not have to change jobs, or even change companies. Keep this in mind when you look at work.

Mind the Mentors

Related to colleagues are mentors. Mentors may be found at your workplace, or may be someone from the industry you are in, but at another company. Usually, they are someone who is in a higher leadership role than you and will be a good source of advice and guidance with your career.

You may want to share your spiritual journey with them. More so than colleagues, with whom you may compete with to advance within the company, a mentor could hone your career, and may be a better choice for you to tell them about your desires to advance or even what that means to you spiritually.

In a sample of 129 U.S. teachers, results showed that the relationship between perceiving a calling and living a calling is stronger for those with a mentor in their profession. (9)

Instead of working your future out alone, consider talking to a mentor.

School's In

Finally, classmates and alumni may be an untapped source to focus on spiritual meaning as well as a place to seek guidance for your future. Classmates could be long-time friends that you could confide and share with, or they may be simple acquaintances that could boost you in one direction or another. They do not have to come from your class year. Keep your options open.

Like work functions, it's good to go to school functions, celebrations, and seminars, both during school and as an alum. You can gain a lot of knowledge and possibly find the support you are looking for as you carve a path to your future.

From family to work, there are a lot of people who can offer support, but as you look into your heart and see what it really desires, finding the right people to talk to could be challenging. Even if it is not challenging, there are people there who are ready to support you if you call on them. In the next chapter, we will look at the professionals and people at events that you can turn to to help you on your spiritual journey.

Two

Consider a Professional

"Knowledge is power. The more knowledge, expertise, and connections you have, the easier it is for you to make a profit at the game of your choice." - Stuart Wilde

You might find people that you already know to support you on your spiritual journey. However, they might be too busy, inconsistent or not the right fit for you. You should not lose these relationships because chances are any support is worth it (within reason), but you might also consider opening up to someone who can hear all parts of your story—past, present, and future—and help you examine and untangle them. A professional might be someone you are looking for.

Before delving into a consideration of all the kinds of people who might be of assistance, let's start the chapter with two examples of sources of help that may in turn help you find someone to talk to or a way to find your heart with a practice you love doing. The first is conferences; and the second is retreats, spas, and quiet days. These paid events are worth considering as places to find connection and, if the right one, maybe peace away from home.

Confer on the Conference

Conferences come in all shapes and sizes. Some are focused on a particular profession or industry. Others are focused on health and wellness. Some focus on spirituality. Conferences can take place in person at a physical location, or can be virtual—or both. How people meet is changing all the time.

Conferences will gather people who have the same interests as you. They may be in the same industry as you, or share common goals or desires. Conferences are a great place to connect and an ideal place to talk with others and dream about the future, especially if the conference is spiritually oriented.

Industry conferences also let you know the latest technology, the latest skills that are needed and new products to be aware of. You can learn if you are a good fit with these trends. If you are trying to improve talk about purpose in a spiritual context or what is secularly as the "Dialogue with Your Future" to a Higher Power, there is good reason that you may find your passion by attending industry conferences.

Get Away From It All

Retreats, spas, and quiet days are also events/locations where you can connect with people, self, and even a Higher Power. All three invite self-care and connection with others, and often invite connection with a Higher Power on a spiritual level. Retreats can be weekend-long trips to a secluded space in a natural setting. Yoga, meditation, exercise, and other self-care practices can be found at retreats. Most of them are vacations of the mind from so much that is busy in our days.

You may think of spas as a simple luxury, but they can be sources of spiritual support as well. Spas are great places for hour-long to week-long trips where self-care is the focus. You can have yourself pampered in time to rejuvenate and replenish the physical and spiritual you.

Quiet Days are short retreats, often a half or full day, that typically take place at a house of worship or seminary campus. The goals of the day may be to read sacred texts together, involve participants in group meditation, listen to presentations, or simply walk around the event without talking. Quiet time for connecting with God/Spirit is often part of these offerings. On a weekend, it might be the break you need to reflect on your calling.

In each of these three places, participants give themselves the time and the sacred space to do significant inner work and exploration. It's a great way to recharge your meditative batteries and live like a monk for a while. These can also be great places to meet people in the same situation as you and share stories.

But maybe you don't need to go somewhere—maybe you could find and use a local professional to help you on your journey to spiritual purpose.

Be Mind Full

Therapists and mental health counselors are great people to share your story with, especially if you would be helped by sharing your emotions and feelings and how you would like to work on them, as well as exploring how past experiences affect and motivate you now. Therapists can support you with all sorts of presenting issues: mental health issues, emotional struggles, relationship problems, addictions, identity, and more. Therapists unlike most other talking professionals, can help you fix things that are broken or difficult.

Therapists should validate you and your lived experience and help you overcome obstacles, whether those involve work, relationships, or serious trauma. When you think about working with a therapist, think about working with someone over the long term, possibly meeting weekly, for however long it takes. They may simply be a guide. Some social workers are therapists and may be better at finding community resources to help you. Social workers and local therapists are well-versed in the community you live in and can provide an outlet for other places of support and growth.

Therapists typically have to be licensed in your state, and therapy sessions may be covered by insurance. If you wish to find a therapist who is covered by your insurance, your insurance provider's "find care" feature is a convenient way to find in-network professionals. If insurance is not a consideration, you can use word-of-mouth or a general search on sites like Psychology Today or Alma.

Proven Professionals

Other types of counselors can also be a source of support. These professionals might include legal counselors, like attorneys; financial counselors, like accountants; or career counselors. These professionals can help plan your future.

Attorneys can help start businesses and create contracts between businesses with your own business if you have one or plan on starting one. Attorneys can also help you plan your future with wills if you that part of your future is your legacy and how you want to share in your savings with those people and groups you care about.

This last part, which can be done by attorneys, can also be done by financial counselors. And to stop now at being focusing on the morbid, financial counselors can help you prepare for things such as your retirement, or tell you how you should invest to start your own business.

Finally, there are career counselors. These individuals can help you navigate the workspace. They can help you stay at your job and advance, or move up the ladder by leaving your job as well.

Making Friends in Finance

Outside of financial counselors, but similar, are financial planners. These people can help you get the financial security to better pursue your dreams. Unlike counselors, financial planners can execute trades in places like markets for either stocks or bonds.

Finding a good financial planner can be as simple as going to your local bank, or looking for someone in private practice that has a good reputation. While a financial planner should guide you based on your conversation with them, before meeting with them be sure to educate yourself on what financial products would make the most sense before you get together.

There are lots of financial products to choose from these days, besides individual purchases of stocks and bonds. There are ETFs, mutual funds and products that support better business as well. You can also invest in precious metals, currencies and commodities, such as wheat and pork bellies. Your financial product purchases make up your portfolio. You should diversify your portfolio and not be afraid to talk about risk and the different levels of risk you would like for each product in your portfolio. Your financial planner may tell you to ignore some investments as well. That's ok, too.

Here's the Energy

The next type of professional is one of my favorites, because I am one of them—Spiritual Director. The purpose of a relationship with a Spiritual Director is for the director to help the directee, or companion in direction, find a relationship with a Higher Power.

This relationship may begin by explaining who or what is your Higher Power. Do they have a name? What is your spiritual past with this Higher Power? Then the Spiritual Director may ask you where you have experienced the presence of this Higher Power recently. "Where was the energy over the past month?" and "Where is the energy now?" are two of my favorite questions to ask when giving Spiritual Direction.

Sharing of stories is also a big part of Spiritual Direction. But with Spiritual Direction, the sharing of stories is not one way. A conversation should take place between the Spiritual Director and the directee. Unlike most therapy, where the goal is to fix problems and the focus is on the client, the goal in Spiritual Direction is to companion with someone and to grow closer in the directee's relationship with a Higher Power.

As you dig deeper with a Spiritual Director, you may ask to find out what your Higher Power is calling for you to do in life. This examination could involve what could be done with relationships, work, home, or family. Spiritual Directors can help guide you with tools to make life decisions and discernment, which I will talk about later in the chapter on spirituality, Chapter Five.

Ethics are important in Spiritual Direction, as well. Although there are no standards for the profession, it is common practice that confidentiality is maintained in a Spiritual Direction session, a covenant is drawn up between the director and the directee before working together and respect is maintained around identity issues be they of the directee themselves or how they define a High Power.

Spiritual direction can involve many modalities. Prayer and the reading of holy texts can happen during a Spiritual Direction session. For creatives, working on drawing inspiration from spirituality is a great way to spend time in sessions. Although spiritual direction is not therapy or a replacement for therapy, it is okay to grieve in a session as well. Individual spiritual direction sessions are often about an hour long and scheduled to take place once a month. Your time with a Spiritual Director can be a long-term or short-term relationship.

Play One for Team You

Another profession that I like to talk about is coaching, again because it is something I do and something that I am trained to do well. Coaches are change agents. You can come to them at any time, but it is best to do so at times of change so you can change holistically on many levels over time.

There are different types of coaches for different situations. Some examples include executive coaching, parenting coaching, and mental health coaching. My favorite is health and wellness coaching because you can take a client and look at underlying health trends as well as the overall wellness of a client. This exploration means you can look at sleep, nutrition, exercise and blood test levels, but also look at work, finances, relationships and even spirituality. You focus on the whole person, and the goal of the client is to look for and create change.

Within six weeks to three months of working weekly or biweekly with a coach, the client should have made planned progress on some level. Coaches provide the temporary support structure to get these goals and visions done. The focus of the coach and the client is to not look at the past but to plan a future based on specific desired behavior change. Coaches can help you find your purpose and work with you to find out what steps you need to take to get the the person you want to be.

People of God

Finally, I would like to talk about clergy. Religious leaders can help you find your way wherever you are in life. They are a great resource for questions about marital counseling, major life decisions, and how to live a more religious and spiritual life. They provide spiritual and religious care. They can help you find the resources to connect to a Higher Power and the discipline that may go along with it. They are keepers and givers of spiritual gifts and can be good friends. I found time spent with clergy and clergy-in-training in my own seminary experience to be refreshing, and it's been a joy to maintain those relationships over time and place.

Making Decisions

"We confess that we have sinned against you in thought, word, and deed, by what we have done, and by what we have left undone." - Book of Common Prayer

We make decisions every day. Every good leader, be it a business or political leader, any good leader, makes a role out of making decisions. If we want to follow God's role for us, we need to make decisions about ourselves and the lives we live.

Political science studies decisions. Sometimes these decisions are historical decisions, such as one to start a country and break away from a monarchy thousands of miles away. But if you study political science well and deeply, you would know there can be a politic to almost everything. Every choice has an effect. Sin, for most Christian Confessions, talk about sinful decisions, things "done [and] left undone." This does not imply that all decisions are sinful, but that the decisions we make are connected to our relationship with God. These decisions have power and its can be as part of a powerful relationship that you have with a Higher Power or God.

How are you going to make decisions? What are you going to do? What are you not going to do? In an age where we are seen both virtually and in person in so many ways, you should be aware of how you are coming across to others, both personally and professionally. You should be aware of brand "You" and the decisions that make up "You."

You are the leader of brand "You." Who are you and how you are going to come about being the brand you envision? What does brand "You" do? How does brand "You" influence your purpose or calling?

Chapters One and Two in Part I of this book encouraged you to take inventory of the potential supports—particularly people—available to you. Part II is concerned with making decisions, exploring topics such as money and spiritual discernment.

Chapter Three will look at the role money plays in your spiritual journey and ways that you could approach saving and spending it. Chapter Four covers discernment—how to make decisions, spiritually and practically, and in combination. We will also look at what that means for us as decision-makers. Remember, though, no matter what you decide and how you live your life, you are responsible for the decisions you make.

We've put it off long enough. Let's start with money and what that could mean spiritually.

Three

Money's a Matter

"For where your treasure is, there your heart will be also." -
Matthew 6:21

We use money to buy services, products and things that we need. Basic economics looks at the buying and selling of goods and services. That field of study measures wants and needs. Spiritually you could try to go solo, but years of ancient spiritual work has shown that what is required in some form is a teacher and a student. If you are a student, you are going to have to acquire money for your learning, even if most of that money doesn't go to a teacher. You will have to spend at some point.

It is also advised that you should avoid going into debt. It is a good principle that you shouldn't spend more than you earn. Romans 13:8 reads "Let no debt remain outstanding, except the continuing debt to love one another, for whoever loves others has fulfilled the law." It is important to be responsible with money.

Moreover, not all of your money should go toward supporting your spiritual journey. As much as books, retreats, and spiritual direction sessions don't come out of nowhere, only some of the money that you earn should be set aside for spiritual practice. Becoming more spiritual is not an all-or-nothing endeavor. In a Judaeo-Christian creation myth, God worked for six days but only rested and practiced self-care on the seventh day. It's important to think this way not just about time but about budgeting money for spiritual purposes and products. Spiritual spending is not for everyday stuff. It should be spent just for the self-care portion of life.

Have you heard of "tithing," typically in the context of church? When you earn money, it might be your current practice to budget your earnings so you know how much you can spend and how much you can save for the future. One of the first steps in creating that budget is to put God first. Once you figure out how much you've earned, it is important to set aside ten percent of your earnings for God. This ten percent or tithe can include money given to a church, but it also can be money set aside for charitable or spiritual pursuits.

Even if some of that ten percent doesn't go directly to someone like a spiritual director or to a House of Worship, making the intention to support a related charitable cause in honor of a spiritual direction session or for a prayer practice done over a week or month, is important, too. It is the giving of gifts that puts meaning to the practice and ritual you engage in. The intention of gift-giving speaks spiritual volumes, more so than giving money for influence or investment. More about this in the next chapter.

Moreover, tithing can be done in many ways. It doesn't need to translate into dollars when you are being spiritually intentional. It doesn't have to go to a church. Any spiritual, religious, or charitable use could be considered part of a tithe. Buying this book can be considered part of your tithe as well! You might also consider setting your tithe aside for going on a retreat, as well.

You can also volunteer as a part of your tithing. Your time volunteering doesn't have to be at church-related functions. Serving your community can be done in many ways. There are soup kitchens, tutoring programs, and clean-up crews that need your help out in the world. Taking up your valuable time to help others for free is intentional and charitable. You shouldn't knock volunteering. It has its place and may help you find your purpose by trying different things.

What money can do is exciting, but the simple act of giving increases spirituality as well. Megan Driscoll explained that based on MRI results, scientists have found that compassion makes the same part of our brains go into action as pleasure does, and giving gifts lights up just as much or much more than as receiving gifts. (10) She then goes on to quote a study in which people who were given a sum of money felt better if they spent some of that money on others, compared to those who only spent money on themselves. (11)

Being more spiritual is also beneficial to your wallet and the wallet of your doctor. Two studies with meditation show this phenomenon. Medical costs were less for a group of people who meditated in a hospital compared to a control group in that hospital. Moreover, Acute Respiratory Infection (ARI) costs were less for meditators with ARI compared to non-meditators with ARI. (12)

However you do so, be it volunteering or giving money, tithing ten percent of your income should be the general rule. The intention and practice is most important. Whatever you decide, money's a matter and what you do with it is between you and God.

Four

Discernment

"Respond to every call that excites your spirit." - Rumi

In the last chapter, we briefly discussed the concept of being intentional, and we used the example of money as something you can be intentional about. You can be intentional about other things as well, especially in a religious or spiritual manner. It's not about making decisions to do things just for the sake of doing them. It's about putting purpose and meaning into the choices you make.

Being intentional also doesn't mean making a decision and following through with it to completion right away. It's about making a point. It's about making a decision that is filled with meaning and purpose—a decision that can be filled with love.

Performing a ritual or saying a prayer before taking action is a great way to be intentional. In fact, the book *How God Works: The Science Behind the Benefits of Religion* by

David DeSteno tells of a study where two groups of people were trying to lose weight. One group took their food, cut it up and then tapped each piece of food before eating it. The control group just cut up and thought about their food before eating it. The group that performed the ritual before eating consumed fewer calories and less food than the group that just thought about the food before eating it. (13) Being intentional is spiritually important, but what about discernment, which comes after being intentional? Let's focus on that next.

Discernment in its traditional sense means weighing the good and the bad, the positive and the negative, and the dark and the light. It's about listening to yourself and listening to yourself well. Remember the question, "Where is the energy?" Through discernment you can make spiritual and practical decisions—just remember that you are responsible for the decisions that you make.

When posing a question that you would want to ask yourself and God, listen to yourself. Try to make sense between the thoughts and feelings that you should pay attention to and the thoughts and feelings that will distract you from being closer to a Higher Power. Pay attention to each decision—each in its own way. What would God want you to do in this situation? Is the feeling you feel related to something you aspire to in your journey overall, or is it something you can achieve now? It is important to be practical, too.

When in discernment, you should be comfortable with yourself and how you analyze yourself in this process. It's important to stay centered and to stay listening. Every question doesn't have to be answered right away. The goal is to aspire to have a closer relationship with God. If you don't pray the conversation, then maybe contemplate and meditate on the conversation. Listen for Him. He should relate to you in the state you're in. Don't be upset if you don't feel comfortable at first. It could take time.

Do note that listening to yourself in a deep and analytical way can be emotionally taxing. Those in spiritual direction call an extended period of being tired in prayer and meditation, as "The Dark Night of the Soul." "The Dark Night" can be temporarily depressing and definitely not enjoyable, but that state should clear up in a day or even hours. Like exercise, spiritual exercise can be taxing. However, this depression experienced in "The Dark Night" should not be carried on for weeks. If the depression goes longer than a day, you should consider talking to a therapist about the depression.

As much as extended prayer can be negative spiritually, the profound experience that most people come out of "The Dark Night," should prove that although emotionally draining, the process of talking to a Higher Power can be good for spiritual change. It puts meaning and a sense of accomplishment with it. Spiritual resilience from prayer is a great quality to hone over time.

When in discernment, what should you ask yourself? Listening to things that bother you, things that need to change in the world or your life can be a way that God is helping you find your purpose. Use that motivation to empower you and change that negative into a positive. (10)

You should listen to your dreams as well. How you want to be a change in the world can be explored and asked in discernment. The excitement that comes from thinking about doing the things you've always wanted to do is healthy. Your desires can be work related, but they could include working on your health, traveling, or building up for a purchase you've always wanted to make.

How should you ask God for guidance? Again, it is best to be with someone else on this journey. But there are several steps that you can take together or alone. Below is a form of prayer that goes across many spiritual practices. Use it as a guide and consider it one of many.

Consider before starting prayer to breathe first. Focusing on your breath for spiritual clarity is an ancient practice in early Christianity, Taoism, and Buddhism. Breath-work is a practice across traditions. The God of the Israelites and later on the Christians was a God of the Most High, found on the mountaintops, in the air surrounding the Arc of the Covenant as Moses traveled across the desert. By focusing on the breath, we make space for a Higher Power to enter into our lives. It is important to fill yourself with the Spirit, ruach or breath.

Besides the breath, we have to pay attention to the mind and our consciousness. It is important to use our minds to think through issues. God's Word comes to us not only through texts when read but through consciousness. God's truth comes about from God's Word. What's challenging is ensuring that what you are conscious of is God's Word. Thoughts come in and out of our heads all the time. We need to listen well to know what God is communicating with us.

While you are listening to what your head is telling you, you should pay attention to the energy that is building up in your heart and what you are feeling as well. Your heart can also connect you to God. You should focus on your heart energy to listen to the advice of God when you breathe. It should be no surprise if the two work in tandem.

Besides breath work and meditation, writing things down may help you discern issues you come across. You can make lists for comparisons, pros and cons that can help you ask what is good or bad? Positive or negative? Dark or light?

Journaling thoughts, prayers and meditations may be helpful to discern life issues as you come up across them. It is also a good way to reflect on contemplations and experiences you have had spiritually.

When it comes to discernment, you can ask God anything: questions about your relationships, your career, your future, almost anything you can think of. You are a spirit with free will. Your decisions are your own, but a Higher Power has a plan for you— a calling. We'll explore that in Part Three.

Introducing Spirituality

"To the mind that is still, the whole Universe surrenders." - *Lao Tau*

Now it is finally time to talk about spirituality and spiritual practices. Even though we touched on this topic in the last chapter by introducing discernment, with some discussion of spiritual discernment, I purposely put the topic of spirituality toward the end.

But what about putting God first and being intentional and all that? By putting people in your life first and then helping to learn how to make intentional decisions, possibly with them, you are set up for spiritual growth in the best possible way. I felt it would be more important spiritually to do that than just going over spiritual practices that you could take on. We needed background before we got into the weeds.

What Is Spirituality?

Spirituality is the quality or state of being concerned with religious matters or being an intentional disciple. Having a relationship with God is important. God wants to have a relationship with you. God has chosen you to grow and connect with, and you are made in God's image.

By looking at religion one can find more about spirituality and what separates the two concepts. With religion, there are four elements found in the four major global religions. Vision, Liturgy, Ethics and Spirituality are these four elements. Vision includes the view of reality of a religion and consists of aspects such as theology, anthropology and cosmology. Liturgy is the relationship between community and God. Ethics is the relationship between individuals within a community and Spirituality is the relationship between the individual and God.

Spirituality has several elements of its own. Intentional practices, or ascesis are elements used to train the spirit. These practices include fasting, vigils, chanting and other verbal repetitive patterns, silence keeping, kinetic exercises such as walking, mediation and concentrating on the breath.

Spiritual texture is important too. It includes your relationship toward God, emotions toward God, whining, complaining and moaning are acceptable too. You can't express yourself this way most times, so in sacred space it is good to let out all of the negative energy.

Mysticism is another important part of spirituality. Being a mystic means that you have some particular vision or image of God and have the necessary gifts to communicate these insights to the rest of us. Mystics can be either Explorers or Exemplars, where explorers take us to the edge of what it means to be human and exemplars "set patterns" for our own spirituality. An example of an exemplar is Saint Ignatius of Loyola, who gave us The Spiritual Exercises.

By being more spiritual and connecting on an individual relationship with a Higher Power one can ask for guidance for purpose. This dialogue with your future can help you find out what you need to do next, especially is one discerns within that dialogue. Sharing your individual relationship with others only strengthens your relationship with a Higher Power.

The Benefits of Spirituality

Even science is saying that having a relationship with God is important. Better health outcomes are linked to both faith in something greater than oneself, religion and spirituality. As mentioned in the first citation in this book, having increased religiosity and spirituality has even been linked to increased resilience when living in difficult neighborhoods.

I should note that being spiritual is important, but in my opinion, being involved with a congregation of some sort is important, too, and the two often work in tandem. Increased spirituality, especially attending a religious service, increased physical health in the following ways for a population study of nursing home-dwelling elderly: "increased spirituality showed lower rates of coronary disease, emphysema, cirrhosis, and suicide, lower blood pressure, lower rates of myocardial infarction, improved physical functioning, medical regime compliance, and self-esteem and lower anxiety and health-related worries one year after surgery in heart transplant patients, reduced levels of pain in cancer patients, better-perceived health and less medical service utilization and decreased functional disability." (14)

Another study on spiritual practice and addiction found, "Preliminary evidence showed that daily spiritual experience is related to decreased total alcohol intake, improved quality of life, and positive psychosocial status." (15)

"Those with strong religious beliefs tend to smoke less, drink less, and avoid substance abuse. It's also true that greater religious engagement makes people more likely to see a physician." Moreover, "when the Pew Research Center [examined] many of the world's largest databases to study the link between religion and well-being, it found that more people in the United States who actively participated in their faiths reported better health than did those that were less engaged or were entirely unaffiliated with a religion." Increased religiosity is related to increased longevity. (16) Being more Religious and Spiritual (R/S) has been linked to increased immune competence by several biological indicators, (17) cancer reduction, (18) and better mental health. (19).

So being more spiritual improves one's health, but being more healthy also improves one's spirituality. It is important to eat right, exercise and do so regularly. The Latin word *spiritus* (spirit) can also be translated as breath. When we exercise vigorously, we do a bit of a cleansing of our bodies with our breathing. Our metabolism increases and our cells digest and excrete more often. We live more and that is good for the heart and good for the Spirit.

Health is important for a person to live a better life, but when you live a life as a healthy person be it mentally healthy or physically healthy, you can accomplish more in life, increasing the chances of finding your purpose and following through with it.

Five

How Can We Be More Spiritual?

"Love is the inner light in everyone and everything." - Ram Dass

There are several practices that one can take to incorporate a greater spirituality in their life. Being more spiritual is important not only as a mechanism for finding one's purpose and calling, it can be a tool kit for getting to that goal that will take you from point A to point B. Discernment and breath-work, both of which we've discussed previously, are important.

We discussed focusing on the breath and its importance. Now lets get a little deeper. Below is an example of a breath practice that you can take with you on your spiritual journey. It can relieve stress and bring about peace and energy.

This particular breath practice is to encourage focusing on the heart, (again, "Where's the energy?") as well as reducing stress and decreasing anxiety. It is called the Box Breath technique. This practice involves breathing into the base of the lungs for a four-count, then holding your breath for another four-count, breathing out completely for a four-count and finally holding that exhale for an additional four-count. After that cycle is complete you can repeat the process over again, as needed.

Meditation or mindfulness are another helpful practice. There are guided meditations on apps and YouTube, which have a person talking you through or guiding you on a meditation for a few minutes. When you do guided meditation, you listen to the recording, following what it says as you listen to it. The focus of the meditation is usually on a word or topic. In addition, the mediation usually has soothing music and sounds to listen to.

You can also meditate by yourself, by picking a mantra or word to say over and over for meditation. One example of this type of practice is the I AM meditation, in which the person meditating says the words I AM over and over, as needed. I AM is how God introduced himself to Moses, when appearing in a burning bush, later asking him to take his people out of Egyptian captivity.

Then there is guided imagery. The difference between guided imagery and guided meditation is that guided imagery asks you to create scenarios and focuses on having your energy flow from one part of your body to another. You could be asked to use your imagination when listening to a babbling brook or birds on a recording. Guided imagery is more expansive and creative. Both can clear the mind and make room for internal peace.

I've provided an example of guided imagery here. It is a great way to relax yourself and when done repeatedly can increase the chance to go to sleep. Lying down, first image that a recorded voice is telling you to inhale and tense up your right arm and release the tension on an exhale. The recorded voice may then instruct you to have the same process of inhaling with tension and exhaling, but this time using the right leg. The practice of inhaling and tension and exhaling and releasing should happen again with the left leg, the left arm, the head, and finally the whole body simultaneously. You can then do this cycle again until you feel relaxed or until you fall asleep. This particular practice is a good way to let your body relax while lying down in bed so you can have better sleep.

These practices using meditation and prayer are sometimes called mindfulness-based interventions (MBIs), and historically they have helped health management and general self-development. Several studies showed that they improve psychological maturation and other competencies associated with leadership effectiveness (20, 21, 22). As a result, many executive professionals today are increasingly exploring the use of mindfulness meditation and other forms of MBIs.

Prayer is another spiritual practice you can incorporate into your life. In fact, you can talk to a Higher Power in any way you would like. There is no one right way to pray and there are many ways to practice prayer.

One person asked me if they could pray every time they came to a toll booth on their way to work and yes, that is an acceptable form of taking time out for prayer! What's better was that a ritual was made out of it.

When can you pray? Any time is a good time, but to be more spiritual requires a regular ritual of it. Examples of this type of ritual include Morning Prayer, Evening Prayer and praying before meals. As described above and earlier in the book about the importance of being intentional, having a ritual or even attempting to have a prayer ritual throughout the day should bring better benefits to getting to the purpose and calling you desire to achieve.

What can you pray about? Almost anything, but most prayers focus on thanksgiving, forgiveness and praying for others in need. Another practice of prayer across cultures is praying to ancestors. You can pray to them for guidance. This may help with finding a purpose to ascribe to. Although not true in every case, the past is often a window into our future. You can also pray for what you want. "Ask and you shall receive" is an important part of prayer. This type of prayer is a great way to introduce dreams you have about your future and what you want out of life. This type of prayer can also keep you resilient and ready for any adversity.

Prayer can include contemplative prayer, which is like meditation in that the prayer is not a conversation, but the repeating of a word over and over again, or following a stream of consciousness in your head that is probably not linear. The I AM prayer above is an example of contemplative prayer.

Prayer can be a conversation with a Higher Power. Prayer can be praise. Prayer can be thanksgiving. Prayer can be a confession. However you decide to pray and what you decide to pray about, try to be intentional and incorporate prayer into your life. It is a great ritual practice.

Another way of being more spiritual is by reading sacred texts. These texts are usually long and could take years to fully read, but like prayer, there are many ways to go about reading them.

You can open a Sacred Book and pick whichever verse comes to you first. You could read it in some sort of order, such as Gospels first or Psalms first, whichever you feel most comfortable. You could read a verse in order or not in order, but consider meditating on it after you read it. Instead of meditation after a verse, you can write about your experience in a journal or some other manner for reflection. Engagement in sacred text is varied. Let's look at a few more ways to stay engaged.

Creatively using sacred texts can also be done. The practice of reading a text and imagining yourself there in the story, either as a person in the story or even as a fly on the wall, is a practice that is often incorporated when reading texts with a Spiritual Director. This type of practice, called Ignatian contemplation, makes the reading of the sacred text fun and engaging. It is a great way to change up your reading of holy scripture.

Practicing patience is another way to increase spirituality and get to the goals that you desire. It also increases empathy and forgiveness. The simple act of waiting could be seen as a form of kindness. In Christianity, as followers explore Mary the Blessed Mother of Jesus more intently, they have found that as a disciple of Jesus, compared to the other disciples, she waited more for her Son to fulfill his destiny. She also waited for his birth. Both women and men can learn a lot from being more like Mary and follow her example.

Another way to be more spiritual is to engage in retreats, spas, and quiet days. Retreats are usually held at a "get-a-way" location, where people can relax, converse and pray on the topic or theme of the retreat. Spas are similar but may have more physical forms of self-care, such as stretching, yoga or massage. Quiet Days are a few hours that are spent at churches or retreat centers, where most of the time people listen to sacred texts and lectures, but then walk around or sit in silence trying to get closer to a Higher Power.

All of these are times at a location, physical or virtual, to meet with people to relax, share in conversation, self-care and possibly prayer.

It is important to be spiritual. Being intentional about being spiritual can help you find out more about what you want to do. Being more spiritual means listening to your heart and seeing what it wants to do. God will talk to you in prayer and God will talk to your heart. Using the techniques of discernment in Chapter 4 and the tools in this chapter should help get closer to God and find out what He wants you to do more spiritually.

Six |

Finding A Spiritual Director

"Seek first to understand, then to be understood." - Stephen Covey

So you want to be more spiritual. You want to take the practices of Chapters Four and Five and put them into motion hoping to find a purpose. But don't forget Part I of this book. It is important to not do these practices alone.

Outside of the ritual found in everything from a church to a yoga class, you might just want to find your personal conversation with God and get closer to Him in your daily life. Spiritual Directors can fill out that void well.

Spiritual Directors come from all walks of life, from every denomination and spiritual training, from every gender and gender identity. Some of them companion you for free; most charge a fee. Most have training, but anyone with a pulse could be a spiritual director. If you can find someone to talk to about your relationship with a Higher Power and you share in that journey, you may have found a spiritual companion.

However, when Saint Teresa of Avila was asked whether she would want a spiritual director who was more spiritual or one who was more educated, she said she would prefer an educated one because an educated spiritual director has more rigor and tools under their belt to work with someone than someone that was more content with life and at peace.

Keeping this in mind, and having all these choices, if you want to find the right spiritual director for you, you are going to have do some research. Know that it's okay to shop around.—Most people do.

Spiritual Directors International (SDI) has a website with a searchable database of member spiritual directors. The website has many filters you can use to narrow your choices down and find the right directors to have introductory meetings with. Besides SDI, the Internet has other websites with databases of spiritual directors. If you are not satisfied with SDI, you can search for these websites.

You can also approach religious organizations, such as churches, to ask who they recommend for a spiritual director. Usually, they can help, especially if you tell them you are looking to find your calling and purpose and want God to be a part of that decision. Again, don't be afraid to shop around and find the one that is the best match for you.

Spiritual Directors are unique from therapists, social workers and coaches. One difference is that spiritual directors often meet less frequently—an hourlong meeting once a month is typical. As much as you may be excited to be more spiritual, the practice should be seen as occasional self-care for most people. Once a month with a spiritual director is like going to church every week, but only on Sundays instead of every day. In both cases there are times when you may want to engage in spiritual practices more, but like going to church only once a week, a general rule for having a spiritual direction session is once a month for an hour.

If you do Spiritual Direction as a group with a Spiritual Director as a facilitator, meeting more often may be the case, so everyone in the group is heard and has a voice.

Another way that spiritual directors are different than therapists, social workers and coaches is that a spiritual director should challenge you. The questions they ask, unlike motivational interviewing of a coach, where positive psychology is used to build up for behavior change, or a therapist where they try to fix past grief and current pathologies, a spiritual director does not try to fix things and would be more honest in their questioning—challenging your relationship with God, challenging your ethics, pushing you to spiritually grow, even if that growth doesn't mean change in your life or religious faith. Mostly they are going to expect you to be frank. "Where's the energy in what you are bringing up?" is a common question. You really have to listen to yourself to answer them.

A Spiritual Director is also often more open with their relationship with you. Unlike coaches, therapists, and social workers, a spiritual director may companion you—sharing stories and talking about their own spiritual journey. A kind of friendship may form. Again the emphasis here is that you are not to find God alone. You can get closer to God by intentionally talking to someone about your relationship with God.

More than the sharing of stories, spiritual directors can spend time with you meditating over spiritual texts and aiding you in discernment. They can pray with you and talk to you about the challenges of your prayer life.

There are also specific sacred practices that you can do with a spiritual director. One of them is the Lectio Divina. In this practice, a sacred verse or line from a poem is read four times. It is a process of meditating on scripture in a way of embracing the scripture from all angles and then letting it go in the final reading.

The Spiritual Exercises of Saint Ignatius of Loyola is a 30-day retreat (with some modern alterations or abbreviations available) that is designed to assist with discernment of God's will, and involves prayer, scripture, and self-examination. It is a Roman Catholic practice, but it has since been shared by many other denominations.

A shortened version of the Exercises called the 19th Annotation, can be done over a year with a Spiritual Director. Instead of thirty days of intense prayer and reflection, only 45 minutes to an hour and a half are asked of a person to pray and reflect each day. It is still a long time. While it is done for a year to get the full breadth of the Exercises, many people choose this option because it can be done even in conjunction with other responsibilities such as work and family.

Creatives can meet with a spiritual director and work with them on creating their craft. Projects, such a song, piece of writing, or artwork can be made for each spiritual direction session. Directees can talk about their feeling and emotions in the work and explain where a Higher Power was present in or during the work. If a directee doesn't make creative work themselves, they can bring in a picture of something or someone they know or don't know, or a poem that they may have written or was written by someone else. Then they can share with the spiritual director where God is in the gift they brought to their Spiritual Direction session. In this way, the relationship with God is explored and grows deeper.

Spiritual Direction is a very contemplative practice. It is not therapy, but it can be therapeutic, bringing structure and solace to people of all backgrounds and life situations.

Seven ▍

Religious Congregations and Clergy

"Prayer in Congregation is Superior to Prayer offered Alone by Twenty-Seven Degrees" - Sahih Muslim 14771

Sharing a ritual in honor and praise of a Higher Power with others or talking with a leader of that congregation can be very rewarding. Most clergy are well-versed in issues that you may want to bring up that are about a spiritual matter, including finding purpose. Clergy can also help deepen your relationship with God. Religious congregations are also a great way to meet people during social time, in study or affinity groups, or doing outreach work together. Congregations and groups can be invaluable in the process of discerning your purpose, and remember you can't go about this alone.

Much can be learned from a group of people with a set of diverse holy gifts. Churches are usually based on a set physical location, but the friendships made there can continue to be a connection, even if you move or leave the congregation. Many congregations now have a social media presence that offers a great way to attend services and to keep in touch over. The people you meet in religious settings can pray for you and you can pray with them, throughout all that you go through in life.

There are other reasons to attend religious services. It is also important to hear God's Word. Again, meditation on scripture while you are listening to it and also afterwards can strengthen your resilience and self-efficacy. Religious services provide opportunities to do that.

Religious institutions also remind us of the importance of confession and repentance. Whether this is done all on one day a year, during the middle of the week most weeks, or every sabbath at the start of service it is a healthy practice, even if you also practice it alone in private.

Music is another great reason to consider attending religious services—some people go just to hear the music. There are jazz masses, holiday choral events, Evensongs and hymn sings.

All of these are reasons why one should turn to religious institutions to find God. As mentioned in the beginning of this book, being a member of a congregation can give many indirect health benefits, as well. And, ritual and intention are a great mix in trying to help you accomplish your goals and achieve the calling and purpose that you are trying to seek.

Eight

Working With A Coach to Find Spiritual Purpose

"Falling out of a posture means you are human; getting back into the posture means you are a yogi." - Bikram Choudhury

Coaches are change agents. If you want to be more spiritual and talk about whatever you have discerned to be your calling and put that purpose to action, coaches are there to do that.

Coaches focus on a client's desired behavior change, even if what exactly needs to be changed is explored in the first session. Coaches will not only look at you spiritually but should focus on you holistically, looking at health and wellness, including career, finances and relationships. Your goals and vision are your purpose, and coaches bring about that opportunity for change.

By laying out goals and a vision, coaches can add structure to your life, even a spiritual structure. Making a Vision of who you want to be in the distant future and determining what Goals you want to work on currently allows you to reach for that future as a positive experience. A coach uses a Vision and Goals and revisits them each session you have with that coach.

Most coaches use SMART Goals. A technique borrowed from the Project Management field. SMART is an acronym, where "S" means Specific—such as a goal that is as detailed as possible. "M" stands for Measurable—so you can make each goal to be quantified in some sort of unit to see if there is progress or regress over time. "A" is for Achievable—where the goal should be something the person being coached can actually accomplish. It shouldn't be too hard, at least not right away. "R" means Relevant—or relevant to the Vision or other Goals that you have set out to do. "T" is for Timely—like Measurable, keeps the goal in some form of time-bound units. Timely also means that each Goal can be projected over some form of time, so in the next coaching session, you and the coach can measure which days and at which times you followed through on your goals. For example, imagine you set a goal to exercise at 5pm on Mondays, Wednesdays and Fridays. It is easy to measure whether you completed the goals. Setting SMART goals can make sure that the goals come to fruition and that they are actually accomplished in a person's busy weekly schedule.

Spiritual SMART Goals can measure how much a person being coached can set aside time to pray or read sacred texts, practice yoga, or even wake up early enough to make it to church. You can have a goal to spend one hour each business day after work on researching your purpose. There's a lot to change spiritually in someone's life.

Other ideas for spiritual goals include keeping a regular practice of journaling, either during or after prayer or reading of sacred text. Finding out what you are praying for and how you can make that more meaningful and more intentional for you. You could discuss with your coach what angers you or bothers you and what goals you can set to remedy that. They can be your accountability buddy. They can keep you on the spiritual track that you want to be on.

Nine

Meeting with a Faith-Based Therapist

"Healing doesn't have to look magical or pretty. Real healing is hard, exhausting and draining. Let yourself go through it. Don't try to paint it as anything other than what it is. Be there for yourself with no judgment." - Audrey Kitching

Sometimes there is more than just meeting with a professional to finding your calling spiritually. You might have grief, abuse and addictions that are preventing you from your need to address being the person that you want to be. If you are dealing with psychological problems, and sometimes everyone does, it might be better to see a psychologist. You may even want to consider a faith-based therapist. While the work of a Spiritual Director or a coach can be therapeutic because it feels good to be closer to God and it feels great to set goals and accomplish them, both practices are not a replacement for therapy. This chapter focuses on the options you have if you need that type of help.

If you need to talk about issues in your life or need to work on mental problems of anxiety, depression, addiction, or anything mental or emotional that's preventing you from living fully, a psychologist, therapist or social worker might be the right person to talk to. If you are looking for a religious or spiritually-based person to work with on these issues, a faith-based counselor might be the person to talk to. Sometimes people in this profession are clergy, but it is not a requirement. Some spiritually oriented therapists may have gone to seminary, but that is not a requirement for good help either.

Any therapist or counselor should see you and validate you and your story, even if they are not faith-based. This journey in finding psychological help can be hard, and like Spiritual Directors and coaches, you may have to shop around. Having your health insurance cover your visits is something to consider, too. Therapists can be in-network or out-of-network and you should be aware of how coverage and payment or co-payment would take place.

Another advantage of having a faith-based therapist is they should not only be well-versed in the scientific core of their practice but also well-versed in sacred texts that you agree with. They also can give you spiritual and religious insight into issues you may be dealing with. These types of insights may not be based on religious texts alone but on traditions in the faith.

Therapists also may know the benefits of choosing goals and finding your purpose or calling. Besides being with you to overcome grief, loss, relationships and addictions, like a coach, clergy or a Spiritual Director, they should be concerned about your future, too.

What is really interesting is that a preliminary study found that religious-based therapy was more effective than standard treatment in mental health care. (23) While these types of studies are new, they are promising and emphasize and reflect people's yearning to have a Higher Power in their lives to effectively recover from mental health issues.

Conclusion

"Gratitude is the foundation of hope." - Megan Driscoll

If you want to have more purpose in your life and become a more spiritual person, you will need to talk to others. Family connections are a great start, but there are lots of people you could talk to, as outlined in the first two chapters. You can always talk to a Higher Power, but I am sure that They would want you to connect with others in some way, as you go on your journey, too. Reading this book may be the first step in connecting with others on a spiritual level. Go for it.

Decisions about money and looking at your heart and mind through discernment are just two tools outlined in this book. Before you choose to follow your path to your purpose or calling, you should ensure you have the tools to move forward to a better life.

Let's look at another Biblical major case of discernment. A heavy topic you should think about after you read this book.

In the Hebrew Bible, Jeremiah 17:5-11, talks specifically about not trusting man above the Lord and not trusting the heart for it is "deceitful." This may have truth in it. It shows the negativity of people. This is a truth and this is real.

But, the Gospel is true, too. Like it is said in Part One of this book: "For where two or three gather in my name, there am I with them," from Matthew 18:20. Jesus' second commandment after putting God first and loving God with all your heart is to love one another.

What is true? Should one not trust people and discern with their hearts, or should we join together with others and commune with the Lord? Maybe we have another mystery? Another "both-and" situation.

If you put God first and then discern, you can find out which verse weighs more to what you feel is the answer at that time, even if it's not to believe in your discernment. You have free will. Embrace it. Trust in the Lord.

This book then talked about spirituality, the multi-faith tools that you can use to be more spiritual and the specific people you can turn to and focus on a spiritual life. Take these tools and use them yourself. If you are a professional, you can take these tools as well and work on them with your clients. If you take these tools, I hope you also use them and find your purpose, calling or meaning in your life.

I hope I have been helpful to anyone reading this book. Thank you for your time and review. God Bless.

Notes

1. Oman, Doug, and Rachel Morello-Frosch. "Environmental health sciences, religion, and spirituality." *Why religion and spirituality matter for public health: Evidence, implications, and resources* (2018): 139-152.
2. Newberg, Andrew. Neurotheology: How science can enlighten us about spirituality. Columbia University Press, 2018.
3. Oman, Doug, ed. Why religion and spirituality matter for public health: Evidence, implications, and resources. Vol. 2. Springer, 2018.
4. Wu, Wei-Li, and Yi-Chih Lee. "How spiritual leadership boosts nurses 'work engagement: The mediating roles of calling and psychological capital." International journal of environmental research and public health 17.17 (2020): 6364.
5. Palmer, Parker J. Let your life speak: Listening for the voice of vocation. John Wiley & Sons, 2024.
6. DeSteno, David. How God works: The science behind the benefits of religion. Simon and Schuster, 2021.
7. Rushing, Nicole C., et al. "The relationship of religious involvement indicators and social support to current and past suicidality among depressed older adults." *Aging & Mental Health* 17.3 (2013): 366-374.
8. Wiley, Jacob. Spiritual Outreach Methods to Support Congregant Mental Wellness. Diss. Walden University, 2023.
9. Ehrhardt, Kyle, and Ellen Ensher. "Perceiving a calling, living a calling, and calling outcomes: How mentoring matters." Journal of Counseling Psychology 68.2 (2021): 168.
10. Driscoll, Megan. Seeking Purpose: A guide for creating a connection to Spirit and uncovering your life's true mission. Megan Driscoll Consulting, 2023.

11. Dunn, Elizabeth W., Lara B. Aknin, and Michael I. Norton. "Spending money on others promotes happiness." *Science* 319.5870 (2008): 1687-1688.

12. Oman, Doug, and Timothy T. Brown. "Health policy and management, religion, and spirituality." *Why religion and spirituality matter for public health: Evidence, implications, and resources* (2018): 191-210.

13. Daniels, Dharius, "Your Purpose Is Calling: Your Difference Is Your Destiny", Zondervan, 2022

14. Thoresen, Carl E., and Alex HS Harris. "Spirituality and health: what's the evidence and what's needed?." Annals of behavioral medicine 24.1 (2002): 3-13.

15. Lynn G. Underwood, Jeanne A. Teresi, The daily spiritual experience scale: development, theoretical description, reliability, exploratory factor analysis, and preliminary construct validity using health-related data, Annals of Behavioral Medicine, Volume 24, Issue 1, February 2002, Pages 22–33

16. DeSteno, David. How God works: The science behind the benefits of religion. Simon and Schuster, 2021.

17. Oman, Doug, and Lee W. Riley. "Infectious diseases, religion, and spirituality." Why religion and spirituality matter for public health: Evidence, implications, and resources (2018): 153-163.

18. Oman, Doug. "Religious/spiritual effects on physical morbidity and mortality." Why religion and spirituality matter for public health: Evidence, implications, and resources (2018): 65-79.

19. Oman, Doug, and David Lukoff. "Mental health, religion, and spirituality." Why religion and spirituality matter for public health: Evidence, implications, and resources (2018): 225-243.

20. Shelly, Rave, and Nurit Zaidman. "Outcomes of mindfulness-based coaching for managers." Coaching: An International Journal of Theory, Research and Practice 16.1 (2023): 31-48.

21. Spence, Gordon B., and Michael J. Cavanagh. "The impact of three forms of mindfulness training on mindfulness, wellbeing and goal attainment: Findings from a randomised controlled trial and implications for coaching." International Coaching Psychology Review 14.2 (2019): 24-43.

22. Vonderlin, Ruben, et al. "Health-oriented leadership and mental health from supervisor and employee perspectives: a multilevel and multisource approach." Frontiers in Psychology 11 (2021): 614803.
23. Bouwhuis-Van Keulen, Annette J., et al. "The evaluation of religious and spirituality-based therapy compared to standard treatment in mental health care: A multi-level meta-analysis of randomized controlled trials." Psychotherapy Research 34.3 (2024): 339-352.

ABOUT THE AUTHOR

David M. Bullock is a Spiritual Director and a Health and Wellness Coach. He got his first break in media as an intern for ABC-NEWS.com in the 1990s. He has since wrote about space and space exploration, creating the first digital edition on the topic, *Space Lifestyle Magazine* and contributing to the business intelligence website, *NewSpace Global*. While working for *NewSpace Global*, David turned toward spirituality as a topic and attended General Theological Seminary to study Spiritual Direction. While at his work connecting other people to a Higher Power, David met his wife, Claudia. Soon afterwards they sought to be health and wellness coaches and trained at the Mayo Clinic. With that credential they obtained certification with the National Board of Health and Wellness Coaches. As new health and wellness coaches, they created Autonomous Opportunities to help others achieve behavior change within their lives. Both work remotely from home in several roles. Besides Autonomous Opportunities, they perform administrative work for the fire safety company NY Fire Consultants/NY Fire Safety Institute and David does additional coaching for the mental health Employee Assistance Provider, Spring Health. This book is David's first book on spirituality. His other two books include one about the SmallSat revolution, *2008-2018: A NewSpace Primer*, and a children's book on space called, *What Is Up in Space?* The couple are enjoying being new residents to Phoenix's East Valley within the state of Arizona.

For more information about working with David Bullock
in Spiritual Direction or Health and Wellness Coaching
go to:

https://www.autonomousopportunities.com